# ANIMAL ATTACK!

# Hunting with GREAT HORNED OWLS

By Ivi Frick

Gareth Stevens
Publishing

Please visit our website, www.garethstevens.com. For a free color catalog of all our high-quality books, call toll free 1-800-542-2595 or fax 1-877-542-2596.

Library of Congress Cataloging-in-Publication Data

Frick, Ivi.
Hunting with great horned owls / Ivi Frick.
    p. cm. — (Animal attack!)
Includes index.
ISBN 978-1-4339-7072-6 (pbk.)
ISBN 978-1-4339-7073-3 (6-pack)
ISBN 978-1-4339-7071-9 (library binding)
1. Great horned owl—Juvenile literature. I. Title.
QL696.S83F7256 2012
598.9'7—dc23

2011048995

First Edition

Published in 2013 by
**Gareth Stevens Publishing**
111 East 14th Street, Suite 349
New York, NY 10003

Copyright © 2013 Gareth Stevens Publishing

Designer: Katelyn E. Reynolds
Editor: Greg Roza

Photo credits: Cover, pp. 1, (cover, pp. 1, 3–24 background image) John Warden/Stone/Getty Images; cover, pp. 1, 3–24 (background graphic) pashabo/Shutterstock.com; cover, pp. 4–23 (splatter graphic) jgl247/Shutterstock.com; p. 5 Ron Sanford/Photo Researchers/Getty Images; pp. 6, 20 Eric Isselée/Shutterstock.com; pp. 7, 10, 11 iStockphoto/Thinkstock.com; p. 9 Critterbiz/Shutterstock.com; p. 13 jadimages/Shutterstock.com; pp. 14–15 Andrew McLachlan/All Canada Photos/Getty Images; p. 17 Daniel Cox/Oxford Scientific/Getty Images; p. 18 Perry Harmon/Shutterstock.com; p. 19 Pictureguy/Shutterstock.com; p. 21 Jon Sturgeon/Shutterstock.com.

Printed in the United States of America

CPSIA compliance information: Batch #CS12GS: For further information contact Gareth Stevens, New York, New York at 1-800-542-2595.

# ANIMAL ATTACK!

# Hunting with GREAT HORNED OWLS

**By Ivi Frick**

Gareth Stevens
Publishing

Please visit our website, www.garethstevens.com. For a free color catalog of all our high-quality books, call toll free 1-800-542-2595 or fax 1-877-542-2596.

Library of Congress Cataloging-in-Publication Data

Frick, Ivi.
Hunting with great horned owls / Ivi Frick.
      p. cm. — (Animal attack!)
Includes index.
ISBN 978-1-4339-7072-6 (pbk.)
ISBN 978-1-4339-7073-3 (6-pack)
ISBN 978-1-4339-7071-9 (library binding)
1. Great horned owl—Juvenile literature. I. Title.
QL696.S83F7256 2012
598.9'7—dc23

2011048995

First Edition

Published in 2013 by
**Gareth Stevens Publishing**
111 East 14th Street, Suite 349
New York, NY 10003

Copyright © 2013 Gareth Stevens Publishing

Designer: Katelyn E. Reynolds
Editor: Greg Roza

Photo credits: Cover, pp. 1, (cover, pp. 1, 3–24 background image) John Warden/Stone/Getty Images; cover, pp. 1, 3–24 (background graphic) pashabo/Shutterstock.com; cover, pp. 4–23 (splatter graphic) jgl247/Shutterstock.com; p. 5 Ron Sanford/Photo Researchers/Getty Images; pp. 6, 20 Eric Isselée/Shutterstock.com; pp. 7, 10, 11 iStockphoto/Thinkstock.com; p. 9 Critterbiz/Shutterstock.com; p. 13 jadimages/Shutterstock.com; pp. 14–15 Andrew McLachlan/All Canada Photos/ Getty Images; p. 17 Daniel Cox/Oxford Scientific/Getty Images; p. 18 Perry Harmon/Shutterstock.com; p. 19 Pictureguy/ Shutterstock.com; p. 21 Jon Sturgeon/Shutterstock.com.

Printed in the United States of America

CPSIA compliance information: Batch #CS12GS: For further information contact Gareth Stevens, New York, New York at 1-800-542-2595.

# CONTENTS

Words in the glossary appear in **bold** type
the first time they are used in the text.

# DEADLY HUNTER

On a moonlit night, a great horned owl waits quietly on a high branch. Suddenly something moves in the leaves far below. The owl's large round eyes remain still as it turns its head nearly all the way around.

The owl opens its wings and drops from the branch. In seconds, it swoops silently down and plucks the mouse out of the leaves and returns to its **perch**. Then it begins to eat. The great horned owl is a deadly hunter!

Fact Hunter

Great horned owls eat many kinds of small animals, such as mice and squirrels. They also eat raccoons, rabbits, geese, ducks, and even dead animals!

The great horned owl doesn't really have horns. It has tufts of feathers on its head that look like horns.

▼

# WHAT IS A RAPTOR?

The great horned owl is a raptor, or bird of **prey**. Raptors search for and eat other animals. They have special body parts that make them deadly hunters.

Raptors—such as eagles, falcons, hawks, vultures, and owls—have strong wings for **soaring** and diving. They have excellent eyesight for spotting small prey from high above. Raptors have sharp **talons** for catching and killing prey. Their beaks are hooked, which allows them to tear their meals into smaller pieces.

talons

This great horned owl lands
on a perch to finish its meal.

# RAPTOR RANGE

Great horned owls live in many places all over North, Central, and South America. Some live where it gets very cold. Others live where it's warm all year.

Great horned owls usually live where there are few people. Most live in dense forests where there's plenty to eat. They perch on tall trees and watch for prey. Others live where there are rocky canyons and tall cliffs to perch on. However, they've also been found in city parks!

8

Great horned owls also like living near farmland.

▼

# DRESSED TO KILL

Great horned owls come in several colors. Many have a mixture of red-brown, gray, black, and white feathers. Their bellies usually have lighter colored bands, and many have a white patch on their throat. They even have feathers on their feet and toes.

Adult great horned owls are between 18 and 25 inches (46 and 64 cm) long. They have a **wingspan** between 3.3 and 5 feet (1 and 1.5 m). Females are larger than males.

The great horned owl's markings often look like the bark of a tree. This allows it to blend in with its surroundings while searching for prey.

With its markings, a great horned owl can hide in plain sight.

15

# OWL SENSES

Great horned owls have strong senses. Their ears are near the top of their head, allowing them to hear better. Their hearing is so good they can hunt in complete darkness!

The eyes of a great horned owl are large, round, and yellow, with a black ring around them. The large size allows them to gather enough light to see in the dark. In fact, great horned owls see very well during the day, but they see even better at night!

Fact Hunter

The great horned owl can't move its eyes. However, it can turn its head nearly all the way around.

Great horned owls hunt mainly at night.

▼

# SILENT HUNTER

Many raptors search for prey by soaring high above the ground. Great horned owls, however, usually watch for prey from a high perch. They might even walk along the ground while hunting.

When a great horned owl spots prey, its dives from its perch, opens its wings, and glides silently to the ground. Its feathers are soft and bendable, which allows the raptor to fly without making a sound. Most prey don't hear the **predator** until it's too late!

Most great horned owls have 12 tail feathers.

Great horned owls may search for prey by gliding along near the ground, instead of spotting it from a perch.

# WHAT A GRIP!

A great horned owl has four sharp talons on each foot. Two face forward and one faces backward. The fourth faces forward when perching and backward when grabbing prey. This allows the owl to squeeze its prey very tightly, much like a **vise**. The sharp talons kill small prey immediately. However, great horned owls can also kill and carry prey several times heavier than themselves.

The great horned owl swallows small prey whole. It uses its talons and hooked beak to tear large prey into smaller pieces.

After eating small prey, the great horned owl regurgitates—or throws up—the feathers, fur, and bones. These castings, or pellets, can be found on the ground beneath owl nests.

Great horned owls love to eat small rodents, such as mice.
However, they have been known to hunt cats and small dogs.

▼

# OWLETS

Female great horned owls have two to four babies, called owlets, in late winter. The male owl brings the owlets food. If he didn't, the owlets would attack and eat each other!

The owl parents watch over the owlets and keep them safe from enemies. After a few months, the parents stop feeding the owlets. This forces them to start hunting for themselves. By autumn, the young owls are ready to make it on their own.

When owlets are about 5 or 6 weeks old, their parents place food on nearby branches to get the young birds to leave the nest.

Foxes, coyotes, and hawks will eat owl eggs and owlets.

# STAYING ALIVE

Great horned owls live a long time. In the wild, they often live up to 13 years. In **captivity**, great horned owls can live close to 40 years.

The great horned owl's biggest enemy is people. Some die when people cut down their forest homes. Some are shot by hunters and farmers. Other are injured by cars or power lines. However, the great horned owl has **adapted** to many different **habitats**. Unlike many animals, they are not presently in danger of dying out.

# Great Horned Owl Facts

- Great horned owls are sometimes called cat owls because of their large, round eyes and their feather tufts—which look like cat ears.

- Great horned owls are carnivores. That means they only eat meat.

- Because of their excellent hearing, great horned owls can locate prey hiding under leaves or snow.

- Unlike other raptors, great horned owls will eat skunks—despite the bad smell!

- Male and female pairs often stay together for life.

- Both males and females "hoot" like other owls. However, males have a deeper voice.

- Great horned owl parents will attack people who come too close to their eggs and owlets.

# GLOSSARY

**adapt:** to change to fit new surroundings

**captivity:** the state of being caged

**habitat:** the surroundings where a plant or animal lives

**migrate:** to move from one place to another when the seasons change

**perch:** to sit or rest on something. Also, the object on which a bird sits or rests.

**predator:** an animal that hunts other animals for food

**prey:** an animal hunted by other animals for food

**soar:** to fly high up in the air with little effort

**talon:** a claw on the foot of a raptor

**vise:** a tool that squeezes things to keep them from moving

**wingspan:** the length from wing tip to wing tip when a bird's wings are stretched out

# FOR MORE INFORMATION

## Books

Markle, Sandra. *Owls*. Minneapolis, MN: Carolrhoda Books, 2004.

Sill, Cathryn. *About Raptors*. Atlanta, GA: Peachtree Publishers, 2010.

Wyatt, Laura. *Those Outrageous Owls*. Sarasota, FL: Pineapple Press, 2006.

## Websites

**Great Horned Owl**
*animals.nationalgeographic.com/animals/birds/great-horned-owl/*
Read more about great horned owls and hear what they sound like.

**Nature's Perfect Predators: Great Horned Owl**
*videos.howstuffworks.com/animal-planet/36036-natures-perfect-predators-great-horned-owl-video.htm*
Watch a video about the great horned owl and learn more about its hunting abilities.

# INDEX